Carried

Carried

Collected Poems

by

Thayer Cory

© 2024 Thayer Cory. All rights reserved.
This material may not be reproduced in any form, published,
reprinted, recorded, performed, broadcast,
rewritten, or redistributed without
the explicit permission of Thayer Cory.
All such actions are strictly prohibited by law.

Cover design by Shay Culligan
Cover photo by Mohd-Zuber-Saifi
Author photo by Sarah L. Brigham

ISBN: 978-1-63980-584-6

Kelsay Books
502 South 1040 East, A-119
American Fork, Utah 84003
Kelsaybooks.com

For my siblings Chris, Eleanor, Bob and Hoyt

I've never known a world without you in it.

Acknowledgments

Thanks seems a small and inadequate word to express my gratitude for the many people who accompanied me as I wrangled this book into being. But it is what comes. For insightful comments about some of these poems, abundant thanks to Suzanne Rhodes, Phyllis Haislip and Emily Pease. For their ongoing suggestions and trusting presence, gratitude for the members of my local poetry group, *Caliope:* Mary deLara, Janice Hoffman, Linda Partee, Mac Mestayer, Peter Trainor, Louise Sharer, Ed Von Gehren, and Edith Stokes. Special thanks to Phyllis Haislip and Mary DeLara for proofreading this manuscript so carefully. Thanks to my cheerleaders, Cynthia Pease, Hoyt and Lynn Cory, Judy and Shomer Zwelling. Your support and encouragement have meant the world. My four children, Damon Cory-Watson, Vikram Weet, Anna Cory-Watson, and Josh Weet, their spouses and my eight grandchildren are inspirations and always available to buoy me up and keep me grounded. They deserve a standing ovation. Gratitude for the many teachers, poets and non-poets, who have guided and taught me how to live and write more generously, especially Albert Pesso and my aunt, Mary Elisabeth Thayer. Finally, a nod to my grandmothers, Julia Cady Cory and Anna Chittendon Thayer, both poets, who instilled a love of words in my parents, David C. Cory and Constance T. Cory, who passed that love on to me.

The following poems have appeared in slightly different form in *Cracked Open,* a chapbook published by Finishing Line Press: *Epiphany; Opening; Laundry Basket.* All proceeds from the sale of this book will be donated to Baltimore Yearly Meeting Camps, a Quaker camping program run by The Religious Society of Friends.

Contents

Part I

In Defense of Darkness	15
Starlight	16
Epiphany	17
Walking into Day on the Camino de Santiago	18
The Mirror Master	19
First Strawberries	20
Moon Again	21
The Beach Is Not a Life	22
Shedding	23
Inscape: Livingston, MT	24
Rooted Wings	26
Wren and I	27
I Pour My Prayers into the Birds—June, 2020	28
On the Way—Camino de Santiago	29
Montana Night	30
Long Day's Hike on St. Oswald's Way	31
Invitation	32
Opening	33
Tree Down	34
Amagansett: This House on Shifting Sand	35

Part II

Carried	39
God Lives in There	41
Quintin Finds His Groove	42
Visitor at Home	43
Lunch with Violet	44
Daughter	45

Before Thanksgiving—2018	46
Venus	47
Obituary	48
Newborn	49
Birthday Wish	50
Chances Are	51
The Unspoken	52
In the Woods	53
Sparkle Girl	54
There's Nothing Better Than a Dog Park	55
This Morning Wind	57
We Light Up This Day	58
All Things Rough and Bumpy	59
The Past Comes Close	60
For Annabelle	61
The Ending	62
Perfection Angel	63
Spidey Sense	64
Afterwards	65
Three	66
Laundry Basket	67
After Uvalde (22/18)	68
The Homecoming	69
To My Father	70
Simone, Almost Three	71
Dealing with It	72
Prayer on That Day	73
When the Dust Lay Down	74
We Linger	75

Part III

Surely Change Is Holy	79
Beyond Words	80
The Robin	81
Beyond a Guppy	82
After the Funeral	83
Autumn Morning on Long Island	84
Woman Waiting in a Train Station	85
Is It Enough?	86
Disaster Movie	87
What Solace Is There?	88
Visitation	89
Choose Something Small	90
Answer to a Prayer	91
Tuscan Cypresses	92
Broken Windows—Two Views	93
On Hearing About the Death of a Child	94
Making Waves	95
Noting	96
Winged Things	97

Part I

. . . to lose for a moment all that it touches back to wonder
—Richard Wilbur

In Defense of Darkness

Worm in the earth, launched
to the light by my trowel throwing
dirt, hands ripping
weeds, exposing you to death
by sun-bright morning,
you bunch and stretch the thinner-than-a-straw
tube of your body, opalescence glistening naked,
muscled diligence already inching
back to your ink-blind home where you'll burrow
and fill this plot with air.
Tunnels shifting, furrows crumbling,
you'll eat through clots
of rotten leaves and slimed remains
of creatures churning, your feces
fodder for unseen microbes
and half-lives moving in.
Later, I'll read
there are up to seven million
of you for every one of me, and Darwin believed
you were the most important
creature of all. But now I cover just you,
watch you slip into the yielding dark.

Starlight

After the children were asleep,
we slipped out of the house
to find the night
dazzled with stars.

Indecipherable runes,
bare hints of meaning—
the Big Dipper clear
as ink spots on white paper,
the Milky Way strewn
like a path of sand,
a constellation whose name
we couldn't remember.

Slowly we surrendered
our meager knowledge
of the heavens
and were carried away
by those glittering shards
piercing the eternal dark
with their clamor of laughter
and hope.

Bathed in starlight,
our own lights shimmering,
we were drawn together—
a constellation
held in a group embrace.

Epiphany

It was two goats
statue-still
behind the fence
eyes gray
glassy as marbles

It was the tufts
of grass
they stood on
the clumsy sheep
behind them
and the clods of earth
all dark and damp

It was the way
as we drew near
they inched
stupidly towards Tom
and the way
he scratched their noses

that sent the shards
of the kaleidoscope
tumbling turning everything
suddenly precious

It was then I knew
that somewhere deep inside
goats sing praises
sheep rejoice
grass adores its loveliness
and dirt is lit from within

Walking into Day on the Camino de Santiago

Cold remnant of night
battles the beams of our flashlights.
Morning stars wink promises
but offer no warmth.
Hunched and stiff, we shift
our packs, will our feet forward.

When did we see the lone figure ahead—
ink blot on charcoal field?
And when did the warm breath of the world
melt black into gray, create color and form
where nothing was? Now a cornfield,
a red backpack far ahead, a cow behind a fence.

We turn, searching the source of this miracle.
The sun is blushing, as if pleased for our discovery.
It migrates into our bodies. Fingers uncurl,
shoulders breathe again.
We walk into daybreak sky,
pace quickened, bones released.

The Mirror Master

A northern cowbird perches
on a porch chair,
entranced by his reflection
in our kitchen window.
He remains for hours
bobbing his head, puffing feathers,
shifting his weight
as if to get a better view.

He returns each day
while his mate scolds
frantically from the feeder,
perhaps reminding him
New England climes are calling,
their kin have already departed.
But he remains in a stupor,
lost in the visage of his new best friend.

I know him—a mirror-master
snared by soft-self comfort.
He prefers the familiar
story in the half-hidden shallows
of his heart to the terror
of blinking and lifting,
searching frontiers
and sharp edges of flight.

First Strawberries

From green tendrils hugging
the ground, laden with blossoms,
ripening fruit and the knees
that knelt to pick them, the hands
that plucked each berry,
these small dark hearts
in chorus reach up
with whiffs of sweetness,
of dirt, of everything earth.

I don't wait to wash their dust
but devour a handful before I reach the car.
Sun hums inside—glow and warmth—
cloud and fear of frost
lost in sugary succulence,
juice and flesh
transformed to blood and bones,
all knowledge lost,
ecstasy of strawberries
all there is.

Moon Again

oh moon again
whole and haloed
unblinking patched
into winter's night

I search your face
know you know
all there is
you saved me years ago

in silence you remind me
memory goes dark
fear and mystery
come home

oh faithful
you will be lost
and will return
again

The Beach Is Not a Life

The beach is not a life—
all tracks erased,
no trace today
of yesterday's
rivered tire ruts,
foot prints all sizes,
dog paws,
three-pronged fork
of gull feet.
Even wild-haired clumps
of seaweed tossed by the storm
are swept back to sea,
tide-pulled,
wiped like a chalkboard
ready to begin again.

One wants a life to leave some tracks—
an impression in the mattress,
a love letter left in a bottom drawer,
a half-finished puzzle on the table,
even peach peelings on the counter,
lip marks on a half-full coffee mug—
and when it's over, a hollow space,
small or large, a permanent scar
of loss. The sea speaks power of
of cancellation, impermanence its pen.
When I return from the beach
it's evidence I'm looking for.

Shedding

Sun is shedding rain
like an old coat,
dropping it to the ground
with no care for its landing.
Sun shakes itself like a wet dog,
releases a tempest with the fury
of a child having a tantrum.
All day I've watched from the window,
noting how it paused several times
but wasn't finished.
Another breath,
another wave of wet,
sky finally cleared so Sun could break through.
Sun knows what it's doing,
every drop finally wrung from the sky
like the last tears
that leave us open, once again,
to radiance.

Inscape: Livingston, MT

I

The hand of the sun
reaches to hold the lamp
of this day.
Dry-brush clouds
paint fern fronds
on bluing sky.

A bird atop a hay bale
sings songs I mimic
note for note.
Dandelion puffs explode
from dew-drenched grass
like silvered firework displays.

A poet once said,
Never use the word
beauty in a poem.
But what to call this mystery
that steals upon me
like a magic cloak,
erases all the lines,
then knocks me to my knees,
deleting all the words?

II

Imagine a leaf
from any tree.
Lay it gently
into the burbling brook
behind the house

and watch the unspooling
ribbon carry it
beyond the grasp of your hands,
the message on the leaf's
flat surface blurring,
merging into all you don't know,
can't follow.

III

Listen to the choir of green
        rising from the earth.

See birdsong notes
        tumbling through the air.

Smell distant mountains
        dancing on their cold, calm feet.

Taste threads of breeze
        weaving garments of brightness.

Leave behind your bewildered life for a moment
        and settle here into what makes sense.

Rooted Wings

Gone the gauzy green
veils of promise,

the forest green skirts,
the roma red sleeves.

Gone the fading embers
lost in the browning ground.

This is the season
when trees take flight.

Muscled limbs
stretch to mute gray sky.

Bony fingers point
in all directions.

Ah, rooted wings!
You soar beyond imaginings.

Wren and I

Wren, tip-tailed and loud,
brown as a polished penny,
every morning on the porch,
a place nobody comes
where I sip coffee and muse
on the wilderness of aging—
the caprices
of embodied vulnerability,
how easily we become
invisible, left to live
in erasure while death,
like a total eclipse,
begins to realign the light.

But on this bright morning
wren and I remain,
singing with all we've got.
Oh, the earth-dark smell
of coffee, the deepening blue
of mid-May warmth.
Leaf children are growing up
before our eyes,
seeds in their feeders
invite us to live.

I Pour My Prayers into the Birds—June, 2020

I pour my prayers
into the birds,
the every day
visitors to our feeders—
chickadee and wren,
flashing cardinal,
drab little sparrow,
downy woodpecker,
bluebird in regal robe,
nuthatch and cowbird.

I pour my prayers
into the birds
so they will carry
my heart's messages
through sun-drenched leaves
and rain-soaked air,
carry them to nowhere special,
but hold my heart dear
for a moment of flight
into what I love
far from what I fear.

On the Way—Camino de Santiago

The storm tired and finally stopped.
I stripped my rain gear
and drank the luxury of dry,
of warm. I walked on,
at home in the harrowed fields,
the brown world
barren and beckoning,
rocks no longer
battering my feet.

How did I lose my way
or ever believe there were riches
more than this simplicity,
this golden way where
foot falls of the centuries
echoed through my body,
where, for that afternoon,
I walked in love
and never doubted God.

Montana Night

Bugs darted across my headlamp
as I read in bed—
a moth the size of my thumb nail,
velvet gray, spotted pale;
a smaller cousin, soft wings
whipping the air;
many gnats, no bigger
than periods typed bold.

I could have slammed shut
the book, squashed most
of these creatures
without a second thought.
I could have clapped my hands
over Velvet Gray, dusted
them off on the side of the bed.

But I couldn't.
My hands were stopped.
The stars beyond the open window
said *don't*. The brook sang praises,
pleaded their case.
How long have these voices
been searching for my ears?

I turned off the light,
home at last
in the wing-filled dark.

Long Day's Hike on St. Oswald's Way

You say you're *viewed out,*
meaning each lilting hill brings us
to the same summit with its picturesque
village in the distance, its copses,
the same honey fields and the sheep
we saw yesterday.
I might agree—my feet are sore,
hips ache, rain threatens.

But look again! The green-winged hill
is bearing us on its back, sweeping us
into its realm. We are
Lord and Lady of the ancient trail,
Queen of Anne's lace, King of
Morning's glory.
Lakes of simple blue stipple
the darkened sky, slips of sun
bronze every blade of grass.
Wind tunes leap from silken stalks of wheat.

Let's travel here where wishes meld
with Time as it's been given on this day—
same as yesterday, but new.
We'll abandon our aching feet
to the delirious beat rising from the fields
and let the path gather us in its narrow hands
as we glide into the village far away.

Invitation

for CHR

Holy Spirit,
sustainer of all there is,
unwavering, you wait for us
to join you in the work of salvation.

You call to us from our elegant oceans
turning their dark pages,
from greening forests lost to flames.
From marshlands smeared with oil
and glaciers lashed by too much sun,
you summon us to love the world as you do,
to lend our imperfect hands to save it.

As our shadowed lives separate us
from the grandeur of starlit nights,
the miracle of cycling seasons,
you weep for us,
long for us to see, hear, taste and smell
the unspeakable beauty of the Earth,
the glory of the sky,
the sacredness of all life.

Oh, ever-present spirit,
your doors are open.
You invite us in that we may be lifted
from bewilderment and fear
to know your love,
to hold it tenderly,
to pour it into the labor
of healing our planet to wholeness.

Opening

A plodding, patient housefly
trapped inside our porch,
walks a ragged route across the glass,
feels a phantom edge, turns
and like a swimmer
completes a perfect lap.
Up and back, up and back,
a prisoner pacing in his cell.

Suddenly, he hurls himself
into the window pane.
The buzz and hiss
of helpless fury fill the porch.
He stops. Returns
to find his place,
resume his lonely trek.
Up and back, up and back.

Oh plodding housefly!
What blindness keeps you
from the freedom
that you crave
while just two feet away
the door yawns open?

And you, my soul?
Still you cling
in mute refusal,
measuring endless ruts.
Up and back. Up and back.
Could it be
that if you dared to lift your head—
a mere shift of shadows—
you'd find a key,
unlock a love song?

Tree Down

We felled an oak
that sheltered our porch
and watched over our house.
Nuthatches fledged
from its arms, cardinals
and chickadees found refuge there
before swooping to the feeder.
Squirrels gathered winter lunches
in the yard. The dart and dash
of many wings
and scampering paws
graced its faithful form
while seasons, pale and dark
and bright, slipped on and off
like coats of many colors.

For years we lived in sweet embrace
until images of tree-smashed roofs
and flying branches
twisted and hurled us into fright,
made the decision for us.
Now its deep-down roots
and broad-backed stump
will wither, rot into the earth.
Its naked trunk rests—
a lifeless leg stretched long
across the grass.
Soon, the whip-strong
claws of a chain saw
will break it into
chunks of bone,
amber marrow left to dry
for fire to grieve
its final gift.

Amagansett: This House on Shifting Sand

this house on shifting sand
        this cloistered home of clam and conch
                of dune-grass-hidden plover's nest

this stripe of shore   slick seaweed hair
        sun-brined scales and skin
                salt of bone   pearl of gut

where moonlight spills
        on cold beguiling sea
                spattered stars dress night's enchanted page

these heaving waves
        held tight in moon's veiled drift
                like reeling gull   I rise on tidal breath

Part II

I am because we are; and since we are therefore I am.
　　　　　　　—J.S Mbiti

Carried

I

Perhaps I was seven and he fourteen
when he took my hand
and coaxed me into the sparkling Atlantic.
Poised like a gull scanning for fish,
he spied his wave, tightened his grip,
galloped to meet it.
We dove through, kept going.
Beyond the breakers,
way beyond touching
where blue meets blue
in spell-binding vastness,
I clung, squealing, to his neck
while his legs churned in the dark.
I let go, floated, arms spread like wings,
his voice a muffled comfort.

A world away, the beach,
striped with rainbow umbrellas
and ant-like crawlers,
gleamed but did not beckon.
We were anchored where we were.
Soon I shivered, fingernails
and lips bruise-blue.
He carried me back
through crash and foam
to warm sand, full sun.
And then his wave,
the splash of him
running to return.

II

Today, his wheel chair locked,
body slumped,
he straightens when I arrive,
calls my name
as if I were the only tonic
that could revive him.
After hugs and ebullient greetings,
he fumbles for his urine bottle.
I steady him as his quivering arms
muster full strength
to stand long enough
for me to help pull
down his pants and diaper.
I turn away, turn back,
get him settled, zip his pants.
*Well, you see, I really am
an old geezer now,* he says.
I don't argue, begin to mumble
something about memory and meaning,
but he is already trading quips
with my son who has come
to wheel him into
the glorious blue-sky day
where lunch is spread out
on a picnic table.

God Lives in There

God lives in there.
My three-year-old daughter
was pointing at a photograph of a small door
ajar, opening to a storage room
at the back of the National Cathedral.
Rays of misty sunlight
trailed the passage
like the translucent train
of a mystical bride.

We hadn't talked much
about God back then.
We're asking God to bless the baby,
we'd told her at a naming ceremony
for a friend's newborn.
Later, plucking a dandelion, she queried,
Can we ask God to bless this too?

How did she know?
The skin of innocence
thinner than a veil—
light pouring into a forgotten door,
a humble dandelion
shining through her beginner's words,
her beginner's world.

Quintin Finds His Groove

He ignores the toys
and the wrapping paper.
He whimpers, cries.
Boredom? Frustration?

We place a red plastic box
in front of him. His eyes widen,
his ten-month-old fingers
bang the button on top.

Music, rollicking and rhythmic,
blasts the air, finds his body, enters.
Quintin kicks his feet, waves his pudgy arms,
bounces in perfect sync.

He is laughing, squirming, clucking
at his good fortune to be here
in the middle of music—perfect joy
tap-tap-tapping in his baby heart.

Visitor at Home

When he's home for a visit,
he glides away like a hawk
on a wire shrugging its wings
into flight. I want to chase him
but hold back, alert, uncertain what the mother
of a newly-minted man should do.

Expect him home for dinner?
Ask about a love interest he's mentioned?
I hesitate in this terrain; the shape
of him new, the way he looks at me
fondly like an indulgent uncle
who might pat my head
and pull a treat from his pocket.

He sleeps late, there are errands
to do, friends to see.
It was only yesterday he ran full tilt
to reach my outstretched arms
when I picked him up from preschool.
Velcro baby I sometimes called him,
so strong was his need to be with me.

Soon he'll head back to his life,
an adult habitat I know little about,
and I'll be left to coddle
snippets of conversation,
the moment I rubbed his back
while he sat at the computer.
I'll smell his vegetable curry
and see, when he casually bends
to the dishes in the sink,
how his hawk wings shrug
a little as he reaches for the soap.

Lunch with Violet

for Violet W.

Hair askew, gray roots exposed,
she's smaller and pushes a walker.
All the rage, she chuckles,
her southern accent elongating the words.
Conversation, once fluid,
stalls, floats away like dandelion puffs.
Her Reuben sandwich looks
made for a giant. With a sigh
she nibbles gamely, picks at
tendrils of sauerkraut.
She beams at the strawberry yogurt,
retreats into it as she spoons
each silky, pink bite. Every morning
she stands by her bed. *This will be
a good day*—not a wish, a fact.
Her husband visits at night, she says,
offers comfort, promises a reunion.
We glance up, smile fondly,
anchoring ourselves for a moment.
When I hug her
and walk to my car, I wonder
was this grief
or celebration?

Daughter

I sleep in your room now.
I still refer to it as yours
though you haven't lived here for years.

Some nights the skylight,
full of moon glow
and bony branches,
brings you swirling
into the room,
and I see again,
how you emerge
and retreat like a turtle,
shy and bold, wise and tough.

I used to wish
a time-goddess
would hurl us
back through the years,
let us begin again.
Core of my heart,
I'd never take my eyes off you.
I'd want you to know
in every cell of your body
the errors of my childhood
weren't yours.
Never yours.

Now I see you were right to flee—
my precious, wobbling like a child
on a two-wheeled bike,
picking up speed, growing
smaller and more breakable
with distance, but pumping,
pumping for your life,
your coat open and flapping behind you.

Before Thanksgiving—2018

Ten days from now you will all come home,
adult, professional, attached to your lives.
We will kill the fatted calf—in our case
store-bought organic beef, soy milk
for the lactose intolerant, almond flour for the gluten-free.

I will spend days cooking,
cleaning, pulling stroller and high chair
from the basement, removing every
fragile object from the reach of tiny hands.
I'll check the wine supply,
make sure the right brand of coffee
rests in the freezer. We'll move
furniture to create more room
for your ballooning families.

You will read our moods and try to adjust
as you always do. We will all labor to wear
bright faces. There will be moments
when love leaks out unguarded,
as son and son-in-law play guitars
or we delight in a meal, the mood turns drowsy
and even the children find quiet things to do.

So aware am I that you are visitors,
come in the ambivalence of love and duty,
weary of travel and filling holes
of the past, still comforted by the anchor of home,
unsure what you'd do without us.
Are you aware that our circle
is tightening, corralling us slowly
into rooms with fewer doors? Can you imagine a future
where we stumble and you, like parents, reach out
to catch us, tell us everything will be okay?

Venus

Cupped in a smile of moon,
Venus—a diamond
so bold mere stars
take flight.

Named for the Roman goddess
of love and beauty,
they call this brightest planet
Earth's sister. I can't stop
thinking about my own sister

slowly waning into Alzheimer's.
When I was a girl,
she was a goddess,
a star in my eyes,
I her pale shadow.
Now open and innocent,

stroked by loss but not afraid,
she looks to me for guidance.
Love and beauty.
Love and beauty.
I can't stop saying the words

as darkness tilts,
raining diamonds
and slivers of moon
onto my slender shoulders.

Obituary

Watson, Neill Pat III, Age 69,
of Williamsburg, VA,
died November 10, 2016
after a short illness.
He was the son of Neill Pat Watson, Jr.
and Violet Kerr Watson.
He was a quiet rebel yell,
a conformist who broke out of the box.
He was an only child who learned hard
the joys of solitude, the depths of isolation.
He was the swirl of smoky thought rising
from an underground volcano
and the eager flame that tickled water to a boil.
He was *amāvissem*, the pluperfect
tense of *amāre*
and the stacked notes scrawled on the G clef.
He is survived by his four *Honeys*
and three grandchildren.
He is survived by a world
slightly more peaceful
because he listened and remembered.
He remains in the chuckle
floating over the dining room table
after an off-color joke, in *Brown-Eyed Girl*
still wafting from his guitar,
and in his path at the Rec Center pool.
He also remains in the generator
with all its instructions placed in an envelope
beside the fuse box in the basement.

Newborn

Her mother, my daughter, has nursed her
and presented her to me.
She lies asleep on my chest,
new-born ear pressed to my heart,
ancient choral beat pulsing between us.

She rests now, a swaddled miracle
where nothing was,
alive with generations,
past and future,
cupped in her tiny womb.

Birthday Wish

For Damon

The dazzling arrival
of your daughter
has you curious
about your own birth.
No drama, I say. *Long labor,
no drugs and voilà! You were in the room.
After a lusty welcome,
you lay on my chest, silent,
until Dad cut the umbilical cord
and gave you a bath.
You nursed easily, looked around
and slept.*

An uncomplicated first song for a life
grown large with complex riffs
and melting harmonies.
A life divided like a swarm, honeyed
and stung with love and loss,
veined like a vine grown tall
and tangled. A simple start
grown rich and clear, brilliant
and breathless.

May you, in your busy days,
return to the melody
that sent you streaming
into this world—an easy tune
you can always hear.

Chances Are

Remember Johnny? Charlie, the checkout man
at Trader Joe's, asks dreamily as Johnny Mathis
drifts over the loud speaker.
Cindy Fuller's basement, I say.

The darkened room with a rim of light
squinting around the door upstairs
reminding us her parents were close by.
A faded gray sofa, the velvet voice
floating from the record player.
The air close and charged
as we groped toward each other
and he slid his tongue into my mouth.
I shut my eyes against the stars
in his and heard our minister whisper
that this slip of composure,
the way a touch could set me on fire
was wrong. Eyes open, the boy's silly grin
reining me in, careful not to look
or touch his pants, his instinct
to carry us forward arousing pity,
me backpedaling like a circus clown.

But hold me close, tell me again
and again my chances of finding
the one and only one for me,
my heart's valentine gushing,
escaping basement morality,
freed into the magic of moonlight.

Charlie snaps me back to my tote bag.
Was that you in the back seat of my old car?
he chuckles. *Yes,* I say,
chances are awfully good.

The Unspoken

There it is
crouching in the corner,
peering from behind
the dog's lush fur.
Its familiar plea
rises into the commonplace—
your trip to the grocery store,
my yoga class.
It rimes our conversations
with its icy glaze,
hangs between us
swaddled in our daily rituals
and the small acts
of cover-coating kindness
we share. It stalks
insistently, always calling
for the words
we dare not say.

In the Woods

For Sawyer and Roland

Lost in that undivided happiness
of childhood, you Southern California
boys dash through the woods
behind our house, climb
on fallen trunks, brandish sticks
like swords, roar victory
with every leap.

The day is warm
and dry enough to hear the crush
of bounty underfoot, smell
the must of wood dust.
Too often I can't find
my way into that world
where all senses
pulse with joy, and spirit
whirls with happiness.
But today you take me with you.
I'm am soaring
with the beauty that is you
pulsing through the woods.

Sparkle Girl

For Olivia

Hey Sparkle Girl!

I see your light,
your winged dancing
moves. I sense the delight
you feel in your bones.
I know you can't help
but keep me in sight
as twirls spin you
out of yourself
plunging you right
into my waiting heart.

Hey Sparkle Girl!

Don't let anyone stop
you from soaring your kite,
from catching the wind
and lifting your face to the light.
Glow in the dark, toss
your gold hair
and sing into twilight.
Grace will catch you
with its gentle hook.
You'll turn and turn
and come down right.

There's Nothing Better Than a Dog Park

The Hudson rests smooth as sea glass
as Eleanor and I stroll through Riverside Park.
I am collecting memories
the way I collected sea shells
when we were children—
the rare and whole, jagged fragments
all equally cherished.
The woman ahead, in an oversized black coat,
is rigid with intention as she limps doggedly,
shoulders jutting.
Three teenagers, all speed and laughter, skate by.
A couple, tattoo-patched and mohawked,
tilt their heads together, smile.
We stop to marvel at name-tagged trees,
though neither of us will remember what they are.

I drop the bait of conversation,
but she doesn't bite.
Finally, she speaks:
We were raised in some interesting ways,
she muses. I grab the hook. *Remember
Sunday afternoons at Grandma's,
how you and I would lie
on the beds in the guest room
and make up stories about two girls named
Sussy and Bussy? Oh, how we got carried away
by the giggles as we took them on adventures!
Or the time (we were young adults)
you and Bob and I rode bikes, came back
hot and sweaty and got soused
on gin and tonics? What about how I followed
you everywhere wanting to do everything you did,*

and how once you persuaded Mother to take you
and Gail Luccarelli to her house
to escape your pesky little sister?
Eleanor chuckles vaguely, gazes
into the distance. The shells I gather
and store like a squirrel hoarding acorns
have slipped through her fingers.
We walk in silence while the world brightens
and dims all at once. How is this possible?
Shall we go to the dog park? I query.
My sister, a composer whose bright notes
are fading into silence,
turns to me. Her eyes widen, her step quickens
when she sees the familiar fence.
Oh, look at that silly one, she coos,
as a black lab mutt gambols into the park
and runs circles around his pals.
Eleanor has never been a dog person,
but here we are giggling and pointing,
cheering as dogs tumble and chase.
There's nothing better than a dog park,
I proclaim. I glance at the river
which has caught a breeze
and is rippling to the sea.

This Morning Wind

This morning wind
        lifts and blows
                grass in the hayfield

like a hand quick-flipping
        through a bright green book
                words on waves

script so swift
        messages impossible to discern
                erased

as new ones dash by
        only the language of flow
                and emerald except to say

the world's on the run
        and three friends
                gather as they have for years

old and wind-worn
        scanning past pages
                hushed by the rush of time

We Light Up This Day

The jailed light of night
begins its slow release
as you nestle into my arms and sleep.

It's 6:30. We've been awake
for three hours—
you and I and the solemn darkness.

I talked
while you stared at the twinkling lights.
I sang as many songs from *My Fair Lady*

as I could remember
and read you passages from the Tao Te Ching,
which left us both silent for a while.

Soon you will wake in squawking hunger—
a simple need your mother will satisfy,
and I will return to bed, also filled.

But not before daylight joins us,
free at last to be wholly here, bursting
into exultation, as we are, ready to light up this day.

All Things Rough and Bumpy

My mother was smooth
like polished marble,
like a playground slide,
like a seal's back.
You couldn't cling to her
the way a monkey hangs onto its mother.
She didn't leave scars
where you'd scraped against
her sharp edges.
You couldn't drape yourself
over her frame.
She wasn't ragged or nubbly
like dry grass or Velcro.

So now I love all things rough and bumpy.
A cow's tongue licking my hand,
lichen-covered rocks
and knotted root-filled earth.
Car tires and carpet under bare feet.
A crevice, a wrinkled face,
the crenulated bark of a loblolly pine.
Things that catch and hold
like pollen on a bee's back.
Anything that invites me
to feel its shape and fold myself
around it, feel comfort,
know touch.

The Past Comes Close

The past comes close
pressing through layers of time,

pressing until the fabric of my now
thins like the elbow of a worn sweater,

and I feel you again slicing me open
as we plunge down the Allagash,

ignorant of how to ride rough rapids,
only the voice of the ranger

telling us to head for the middle,
defy instinct and logic,

go where the river churns,
where it looks dangerous,

slash our paddles through
the blind water to find that spot

where the cascade parts and flings
itself over rocks that guard

the path to a pool of calm.
We don't hesitate, filled as we are

with the courage and arrogance not to doubt
our fragile selves—the ones that haven't yet

been split and left on the river bank like the canoe
carcasses that warn us to be careful.

For Annabelle

I

Bell chimes through sun space
        twinkling as it croons her song
Belle's music finds our ears

II

Water bug dashes
        down tunnels   dancing rainbows
Bubbles rise triumphant

III

Tree-climbing spider
        Nose-nuzzling acorn finder
Outside girl sees all

The Ending

I thought he would want to spare us
his last frailty—
he who folded every shirt just so
and never missed his days to swim.
But in the last weeks of dying
he surrendered all that
coiled tightness. As time thinned,
sparks of spirit seemed to enfold him,
leaving him pliant as bread dough.
He didn't mind if his girlfriend and I
were there when the nurses came
to clean him or change the tubes.
He sank into the sheets,
protesting only when they asked for effort,
never at his plight or loss.
You have to know how precise he'd been;
careful and deliberate in all he did,
focused on his body, how it looked and worked,
his mind and all it had amassed.
But there he was, almost unspeaking, yielding
as if he'd been given permission
to stop being perfect.
I want to think some voice was calling him
to love the chaos and collapse within,
to abandon all effort,
finally, to be himself.

Perfection Angel

For Desmond

It's a perfection angel,
you announced as you stared
at the sole print of your boot
mashed into the snow.
And behold. There it was—
a circle surrounded by waving wings,
surely the image of an angel.
I'm a Perfection Angel.
You composed a little tune.
You tromped on,
a five-year-old, complete.

Spidey Sense

My grandson has just turned three, worships
everything Spider Man. That web-slinger
crouches on his birthday cake, pounces
across his T-shirt, catches thieves like flies.

From my perch on the spire of years,
I watch his world, spin my threads,
then hurl them.
Gently, fiercely.

Afterwards

We were all in our places—
your husband,
your children,
your two loyal friends.
But you were not there.

We were there as we had been
for those last caregiving weeks;
curled in the recliner, folded
into the rocker, hunched on the bed.
But you were not there.

The body belonged to you.
The hands were yours,
the wrists, the bird-thin legs
forming hillocks beneath the covers.
But you were not there.

The tulips in the yard were there
and the musty smell of the marsh
beyond the open window.
The heron was there, hidden in his grassy home.
But you were not there.

The invisible air continued
to weave its dance through us.
It hovered about you,
peered into your darkness.
But you were not there.

Your husband plucked at the blanket,
pulled it close to your chin
as if to warm you. He stroked
your hand as he'd done so many times.
But you were not there.

Three

for Violet

Those first days when you locked
        your gaze to mine
        and wouldn't look away,

I knew you had claimed me
        and wondered what else
        in this world you would claim.

Now you are three.
        You measure your shadow,
        wing into snow angels.

You are going places,
        books and bunnies with you,
        memorizing, claiming every step.

Sixty-six years separate us,
        but we agree the world
        is a place of serious interest.

We pick up stick brushes
        and paint the leaves blue.
        Fee fi-fiddly-i-o becomes our song.

Laundry Basket

She carries the basket downstairs,
almost hidden by its mound of laundry,
hem of her pale-yellow uniform
barely visible.

I watch—
my five-year-old eyes
held by her dark, creamy legs.
Ruthie! C'mon. We're going to the beach!

She finishes her descent,
puts down the basket,
catches my eye
for an arresting moment.
Finally, a sigh—

I can't go to THAT beach.

Stun-stopped and speechless,
my spine straightens,
brittle as a frozen branch.

A flash through my body—
frisson of knowing
what I'd always known;

her fingers smoothing lotion on my cheeks,
the claw of injustice digging into my bones.
I turn slowly,
follow my mother to the car
while she hoists the basket
and carries it to the laundry room.

After Uvalde (22/18)

(killed/wounded)

Don't lollygag, I say
to my third-grade granddaughter
who's supposed to be getting ready for school.
Her eyes, dark pools of spark, meet mine.
What does that mean?
I explain. She laughs. *No,* she says,
*It's what happens when you gag on a lollypop.
Get it? What's the antonym?*
Buckle down, says her father as he enters the room.

She does. Finishes Cheerios and blueberries,
brushes teeth, finds blue pants, pink butterfly shirt,
the yellow sweatshirt she favors.
Search for backpack and shoes, her ever-wandering socks
and Django, her worn and precious stuffed bunny.
Her mom, queen of ponytails, brushes and scoops her hair,
and with her dad she heads to the bottom
of the driveway to await the school bus,
while I watch from the dining room window.

I will be there when she comes home.
She'll jump off the bus, ponytail askew,
Harry Potter in hand, Django pressed to her side.
Victory on a math test, tales of the mean girls,
haiku by Bashō all bubbling. I'll say, *Wow! Amazing!
Well, that must have been hard. What did you do?*
We'll trudge up the driveway.
She'll complain it's too steep.
I'll remind her it's good exercise.
Her parents, her brother—the day will gather
and fade as it always does.

We will be there when she comes home.
When she comes home.

The Homecoming

For Damon

This child has been with you,
a shadowy figure, a blur outside the fence.
While you grew into your life
and stacked up accomplishments,
she stood in that faraway field,
a silvery possibility, a hovering cloud
that ballooned your heart, made it ache.

On the day you turned and saw her
moving slowly toward you,
it must have felt like the world melted,
all borders cracked, the fence breaking down.
And as she got closer, I imagine
you had moments of fear, like a priest might
before taking final vows.

And then, the headlong rush,
the giving yourself over
as you flung the door open
and greeted her, this beloved stranger
crossing the border into you home.

To My Father

The beach begins to fill
as the thin light of morning
thickens and day settles in.
A jogger, ears button-plugged,
runs close to the shore,
and I hear you ask,
in your softly scolding voice,
*How could anyone choose rock music
over surf sounds?*

A child in a purple bathing suit
giggles out loud as she drips a sand castle.
Waves sip and sigh,
prostrate themselves at my feet.
Sun tickles my arm
as waves grow bolder
breaking closer to my chair.
A spine of clouds lines the distant sky.

Soon my children will tumble
down the dune like puppies let off leash,
filling the beach with the souls
they don't yet know they have.
They'll dash into the sea,
exuberance meeting exuberance,
and I'll see you again floating
beyond the breakers,
at peace in deep water.
I'll imagine you at ocean's edge
throwing sticks for the dog
who never brings them back.

Simone, Almost Three

She drops a spoon
        into my heart
                scoops me out

I give her blueberries
        she gobbles with glee
                gives back a piece of muffin

She dishes out her joys
        her heartaches
                everything she has

I offer her
        my most delicious self
                We feast

Dealing with It

> *I can't even deal with how cute she is!*
> —Anna, on Facebook

Your heart has tumbled into happiness.
Ground wobbles, lines blur.
A trembling wind
swirls around you,
will never fully settle.

She cries. Abundance flows
from your body to hers.
The drawbridge between you
opens. Eyes lock.

You return, unable to speak
of how you've been
swept away, your heart
alone to ponder, to cherish.

Prayer on That Day

Walking past an evangelical church
on the day of her surgery,
my soul had already flown away.
Stomach empty as a shell,
lungs clenched into fists,
legs and hands on robot mode,
the only prayer in my body
pleaded, *Please! Pretty please!*
Please? Pretty please?

I don't believe in a God
who swoops down
to grant my wish, while others
suffer with no respite.
But there was a prayer box
in front of the building
and a little shelf with index cards
and pencils. I scribbled my petition
and stuffed it through the slot
to be read aloud on Sunday morning.

A vague but gentle comfort crept in
as I pictured fervent strangers
holding my daughter up
in love and hope, able to see what I,
in those obliterating moments of fear,
could not imagine.

When the Dust Lay Down

Finally, a claw clutched
the back of your neck,
lifted you, trembling and weeping
until you had no choice
but to pack your belongings and leave.

Away from your tunneled life—
the boot of abuse,
the chains
of your undeserving self—
somewhere beyond courage,
the ceiling cracked,
tectonic plates shuddered
and crushed the ghosts
of convention,
the lonely secrets.

When the dust lay down,
stars crowded through night sky
to watch you, trees leaned close
to welcome you.
Finally, a hand you could trust
reached for yours,
held you up when you assumed
you would fall.
And as you turned a corner
that you thought would lead to the end,
you were surprised onto the only road
you could travel.

Can you say
finally, the Holy Spirit broke you
and won't let you return
to any path but the crooked
way of love?

We Linger

It's stunning how the world seduces us
into enchantment, leaves us begging for more.
We hang on. We linger even as we're being robbed,
even as we're pulled into the passing tide.

Like this morning, after we gazed at a host of daffodils
and exclaimed in unison, *And then my heart with pleasure fills . . . ,*
after his wheelchair didn't run away from me,
and the afghan sheltered his thin shoulders,

we lingered in the gazebo
overlooking Long Island Sound.

We merely wished to be, to be there.
Balm of rippling bay, balm of ordinary sun,
a seagull on a rock. The day unfurled,
offering solace in these smallest joys,
sublime and undeserved.

Words dwindled as we sat and gazed. We sighed
and wept a little for the fullness of our waking.
I wheeled him back, knowing, in these aging days,
the details of our morning would soon
be set adrift beyond the reach of memory.

I won't ask, *Remember when . . . ?*
But they will linger—Wordsworth and his daffodils,
a seagull on a rock, ripples on the bay, a knowing
deeply shared—nestled in the rhythms of our inner seas,
safe within in the fabric of our hearts.

Part III

I dwell in Possibility—
  —Emily Dickinson

Surely Change Is Holy

Wind wrinkles waves,
turns their calm
to sparkling dance.
Yeast enters dough,
fills once empty air
with scent of baking bread.

As sun drinks water
and clouds return it as rain,
as trees lose leaves
then stretch and bud again,
we rise or fall transformed.

Surely when we enter the river
of change we are baptized in spirit,
in certainty of fire turning logs to ash,
of sunrise and sunset every day,
of light flashing across your face
before darkness descends.

Beyond Words

Drumrolls of rain batter the deck,
fill empty moments
with cataract veils
and walloping thunder.

I stare at my desk
where words rise but won't land.
Pen poised. Paper clear.
Minutes shuffle by, get lost.

At last, I yield,
feel walls begin to cradle me,
inviting deeper rest,
free from struggling words.

Quiet grows,
brims beyond my body
into the room, beyond the walls,
out into the softening rain.

Soon I'll drift downstairs
to make a meal—
pasta with fennel and tomatoes,
fresh basil, salad.

We'll rise and go together—
the room, the rain,
the silence
dwelling now in all of us.

The Robin

The robin rests on the fence rail in the mid-day heat.
Like a sentinel, she stands statue-still
while I watch from the porch.
In her home, my friend has fallen,
slipped, she said, from a stepstool while reaching
for an unreachable bowl. The broken rib has healed,
but there's talk of a "mini stroke"
and now she has migraines.
She has borne the fire of pain
clawing her back since a high school accident
almost felled her. A risk taker
who lives with the knife of failure
poised at her throat, she flames fiercely
but blames herself without mercy.
Be still. Be still, the voice of the robin urges,
even as she begins to tremble.
The argument continues while I wait,
not knowing when she will fly away.

Beyond a Guppy

The cat was black,
unmoving on a mound
in the local cemetery,
napping, I guessed, in the summer sun.

I stopped my bike,
curious and casual.
I was almost twelve,
finally free to ride alone,

no grown-ups near,
no place to go,
just me pedaling fast
or slow, loving liberation.

The cat was dead—
stiff-legged, mouth agape,
its menacing fangs and fur still shining,
flies already gorging.

Beyond a guppy or goldfish,
I'd never seen death,
didn't know about the rot,
the frenzied maggots feeding,

the ghoulish face that hollowed
as summer passed and I sped by
each day just to feel
my heart clanging like a bell.

After the Funeral

After
the funeral
with its promise
of heaven
and life
everlasting
all suffering
banished
everyone
sinless and whole

I decide I don't want heaven.

Keep me here
where rain clouds
turn up growling
and regrets storm through
the broken dyke.
I want to be in *this* world
among the ravaged and resilient,
where every connection
comes packaged in loss,
and love has to be mended
again and again.
Here, where astonishment
takes me in its arms,
spins me through snow-locked
mornings that melt to greening noons
and breathless sunsets dance
a tarantella.

I want to stay here
in the world it's taken me
so long to learn to love.

Autumn Morning on Long Island

Beach-fog this morning,
world under a tarp of overcast.
Waves, grim and greedy,
gnash foamy teeth.
Damp's chill fingers
round my shoulders,
force hands into pockets.
The sea's loud heaving
crawls into my chest,
leaves me gasping.

I'm here alone;
husband tired,
children launched,
siblings in decline.
My mind's dark surf
adds mobs of hate,
children crossing borders alone,
bullets ripping through flesh,
our planet burning, flooding.

Autumn. A time of brightness,
the season that knows its fate
and still puts on dancing shoes.
And I, trudging through
my own autumn, ponder
if brighter possibilities
wait to push aside the fog
or if the dance is almost over.

Woman Waiting in a Train Station

My whole life fell apart in a day.
—Ukrainian woman in a train station with a toddler in her arms

Decisions were made.
He would stay behind and fight.
I would try to leave the ravaged city.
This morning we rise
from the table and embrace,
refusing to speak in possibilities.

I take the baby, bundled in her bulky jacket,
to the train station already filled
with wide-eyed mothers scanning,
brows rippled, jaws clenched.
Some were stoic trees, others bone china
teacups about to shatter.
A stranger's hand on a shoulder,
the offer of a diaper or lollipop,
a knowing nod—small sparks of kindness
melting the cold and hard.

Kateryna's eyes soon glaze,
her whimpering protests fade.
When convulsive tears of anguish and rage
take my breath, my sight,
a friend sits close, bounces the baby,
leads me back into the room.

History has woven us a cloak
of resilience. I feel it wrap
around me now. And so we wait,
women in a train station,
travelling together,
comforted and afraid.

Is It Enough?

> *Life wants to be witnessed.*
> —Damon Cory-Watson

Is it enough to caress the wind-wrinkled lake,
      to hear its soft slap on the side of my kayak?

Is it useful to consider the moth
      as she whirs her wings in frantic flight?

Is it worthwhile to bow to rocks
      that have been sunning themselves forever?

Are we being of service if we woo the loon
      who lets us close or the osprey who eludes us?

Is it helpful to adore the pink palms of the peonies,
      their edges already tipping to brown?

We ask will they bloom if no one is here to see them.
      Is it enough that we came?

Disaster Movie

Fog lifts.
Rills of relief
ripple through my body,
spill over the immutable rocks,
sing their way through swirling rivers
headed to the final sea.

What yesterday loomed large
has taken on its proper heft,
my dire predictions melted
in the hands of truth—a doctor's
lack of alarm, the awareness
that the disaster movie roiling in my head
was just an ordinary plot point
spooling its way to the end of the reel.

What Solace Is There?

What solace is there, my friends, what solace?
Winter sunlight shining on bony branches?
Air crisp as the first bite of an apple,
nourishing soup to warm chilled bones?
But what solace for the parents who won't see their child
take another breath, who don't know if the next bomb
will choose their house to destroy?

After gently brushing away
a gnat who'd wandered
onto the page of the book
he was reading, Allen Ginsberg wrote,
Fly away, tiny mite, even your life is tender.
Shouldn't we all feel this seen,
this cared for and protected?

The day is fading and I must go
with it, accompanied by winter branches,
crisp apple air, nourishing soup,
and the inconsolable parents
now at home in my tear-filled sight.

Visitation

You come to me as sadness,
so present in my heart,
real in my tears.
I wanted a sign—
angel wings
or flashing lights—
but now I'm grateful
for the little bird of sorrow
that flutters within me,
that comforts me,
that is you.

Choose Something Small

I give you the end of a golden string/ Only wind it into a ball/
It will lead you in at Heaven's gate/ Built in Jerusalem's wall
                                            —William Blake

Choose something small. Anything will do:
The way the wood grain of this desk
flows like grass on the bottom of a river,
the way some swaths are wider than others,
some years more fecund. Imagine
that tree and all the years of its grounding. Gaze
at the man who felled it with his deafening chainsaw. Hear
the thunder of its crack and fall. Stand
on the root-packed earth and feel its wound. See
the toppled giant being lifted onto a truck,
one of many bodies hauled to the mill. Choose
to gaze into the face of the lifter, his squinted eyes,
the lines on his forehead like the lines in the wood grain.
And what's next? Many people hefting and sorting,
pushing trunks through blades made in Germany
or China or Ohio. Stare into the blind hot furnace,
watch the molten iron ore, the graphite being poured
into shark-teeth molds, workers in protective gear,
the tempering of steel. Move on to the worker
as he trudges home bent and eager
to hug his wife and toss a baseball with his kids
before lying down on sheets woven by factory workers
in the Philippines. Crawl into the body
of the bone-weary weaver as she walks home in the rain,
as she catches the calls of her hungry children. Feel
the rain, warm on her shoulders and the mud
that splashes her thin legs. Watch
as she lugs a bag of rice from the pantry. Admire
the rice planters and harvesters. Keep
winding the string until the ball you carry holds all there is.

Answer to a Prayer

Another morning and I wake
hungry for the joy
that is mine—nothing more.

Covers closed, eyes silent,
breath caught in possibility until
cold seeps in, focus forgotten.

The prayers that lay in my heart—
praise or sorrow or supplication
die in the fist

of my need to be good,
the damage I've done,
how I have nothing to offer.

What do I do with this resistance?
For surely that's what it is—
the tamping down of love

and imagination with cruelty
and guilt—hiding
as a way to stay alive.

Be kind, says the voice.
Kind? Only that?
Only that.

Tuscan Cypresses

> *. . . the labels "mysterious" or "enigmatic" are often attached to the Etruscans since none of their own histories or literature survives.*
> —Smithsonian Magazine

Swaying blood-dark cypresses in line
on distant hill. Spine-straight faithful pilgrims
form monuments to lost Etruscan souls.

Sinuous cypresses,
black-flame sentinels
tall as evening shadows
hide memories
of faintly smiling men—
the ancient race of Etruria
destroyed by Roman reach.

Brooding cypresses
in silhouetted rows,
pillars of forgotten
thought, witnesses
to forgotten words,
the hollow sounds
of echoes ended.

Still new Romans come
to bury and to silence—
on every continent,
from every race and creed.
The spirits of the lost must not be lost.
Their meaning lives
in primal Tuscan cypresses
that hold the flickering tongues,
the slender, endless mysteries
of all Etruscan shadows.

Broken Windows—Two Views

Whose broken window is a cry of art
　　　　　—Gwendolyn Brooks

Holes in the heart of a city
Raw desecrations
Breath robbed
By many knees
On trapped
Black necks

Holes in the heart of a city
Boisterous voices
Freed to paint
Colors brightening walls
Caged birds
Releasing song

On Hearing About the Death of a Child

There are moments that the words can't reach.
There is suffering too terrible to name.
                              —Lin Manuel-Miranda

The voice inside me howls—
random, uncontained:
The wind has turned
many houses to sticks, whale
bodies are piling up on the beach,
altars rise like tree trunks,
the sun will see morning
and you're going to need breakfast.

But words won't be released.
Throat has closed its tunnel.
Tongue hangs idly in its cave.
Only heart opens, bright,
insistent: *Look how Night has closed*
its curtain, blotting every star
but grief.

Making Waves

for years I've walked
and watched

waves bend and break
crash hard

and rise anew
bend and break

to pull of moon
and windy dance

in lace lie down
obedient

whatever can it mean
to not make waves

impossible and yet
I tried so hard

Noting

She asked me to listen
to the piano pieces she'd chosen
to play for her portion
of a family Passover Seder.
I stood in my yard,
phone pressed to my ear
as she began Bartok's Romanian Dance #4—
dark and slow with notes of hope.
Then the second movement of Mozart's sonata
in C major, its tone and bounce
redolent of freedom and spring.

Suddenly the notes stood clear,
alone and shining like a starry night.
Each had been heard, caressed,
placed carefully under my friend's fingers—
wholes and eighths of equal merit,
quiet basses no less precious
than dancing trebles.

Guided by her skilled, obedient hands,
her practice and her presence,
they formed a blessed community
and soared into a moment of transcendence.

Winged Things

That last night in Italy,
we sat on the cell-sized balcony
of our hotel sipping wine,
preparing for the day ahead.
Around us, the dark began to deepen—
hazy sunset smudged
to gray, shapes erased by night gliding in.
Lights winked on in nearby houses,
a laundry line was pulled
into its window.

Overhead, in endless succession,
planes thundered into Rome.
First, a star in distant sky,
our eyes straining to pull it towards us
as it steadily grew into a plane.
When each behemoth bellowed
and dropped, we shuddered,
certain it would scrape the hotel roof
before lumbering on.

And you, with your camera aimed
at their bellies, tried unsuccessfully
to capture the moment
before each plane
passed beyond sunset.
We laughed at the impossibility
as winged things
pierced the darkness
for only a glimmer,
the absurdity of our pleasure,
mouths agape, hands
waving and pointing because of the din.

About the Author

Thayer Cory was raised with four siblings in New Jersey, but feels most at home on the shore of eastern Long Island and in the wilds of New England. After college (political science) and graduate school (psychology and religion) in the Boston area, she moved to Williamsburg, Virginia where she raised two children and helped raise two stepchildren. She and her husband have hiked through much of Europe including the Camino de Santiago in France and Spain. Her work as a psychotherapist in both public and private settings for thirty-five years continually inspires her to see the world from many perspectives, and her involvement in Williamsburg Friends Meeting (Quakers) keeps her grounded in a spiritual community. Her commitment to her four children and eight grandchildren is also a driving force in her life. All these experiences nurture and inform her poetry. Her poems search for the threads that keep us connected to human relationships, to the natural world and to the divine. She is the author of *Cracked Open* (Finishing Line Press, 2018).

www.ingramcontent.com/pod-product-compliance
Lightning Source LLC
Chambersburg PA
CBHW031200160426
43193CB00008B/447